A QUIET
REVOLUTION

EDITION II

*Encouraging and sharing positive
values with children*

by Frances Farrer

with contributions from Neil Hawkes

fh books

Published by fh books

A Quiet Revolution was first published in 2000 by Rider, an imprint of
Ebury Press, Random House.

Values Education: developing positive attitudes by Tony Eaude
Issue No 34, 2004 National Primary Trust report on work in nine schools.

www.values-education.com

The book is wonderful, and should be compulsory reading for anyone who is serious about education. At a time when we need a lot of wisdom about what leadership in education looks like, this is a rich resource.

Rowan Williams, Archbishop of Canterbury

• • • • •

We are all meant to shine, as children do...And as we let our own light shine, we unconsciously give other people permission to do the same. And as we're liberated from our own fear, our presence automatically liberates others.

Nelson Mandela

• • • • •

The future of humanity depends on universal values.

The Dalai Lama

ACKNOWLEDGEMENTS

This book is the updated and abridged version of the original *A Quiet Revolution*, and the acknowledgements are largely the same as they were at first publication. I wish to thank especially:

Neil Hawkes, whose work at West Kidlington has been a beacon for people in many countries of the world; all the teachers, the general staff, the dinner ladies, the children who gave interviews, the visitors who enjoyed their time at the school, and above all the spirit, joy, fun and aspiration of all the children.

The World Spiritual University for the inspiration of the positive words, the silent reflection, the emphasis on peacefulness.

My father, who backed me and enjoyed hearing about it; my mother, who taught me storytelling and loved little children.

Everyone who was encouraging at the time of writing and whose interest in the work has continued.

A special mention is due to Alex Vincent, who was the school caretaker when *A Quiet Revolution* was being written but who has since passed on. His contribution to the life of the school is remembered with affection.

CONTENTS

INTRODUCTION

WHEN THE FULL length version of A Quiet Revolution was published it caused quite a stir. It told the story of the marvellous efforts of everyone in an Oxfordshire village primary school towards a positive outlook, and of the harmonious, hard-working, happy school community they created. Since then, many schools in England and other parts of the world have embraced the same ideas, contained within the educators' phrase *Values Education*. A report sponsored by the Department for Education and Skills looked at the work of nine of them. It concluded that the values education method when properly applied created better social relationships, better self respect – and hence respect for others – and more coherent school communities. The emotional stability of staff and pupils was often commented on.

The original Quiet Revolution described the work in West Kidlington Primary School, where the head teacher who set the values education work in motion was Neil Hawkes. He points out that aspects of this method of working are present in many schools. What made the work at West Kidlington exceptional was the level of co-ordination between all the staff, and the participation of all members of the school community. Everyone was singing the same harmonious song.

What song?

The values education method appears very simple. It is posited on a consistently positive focus which is both the foundation and the boundary of all activity. Staff at West Kidlington Primary School chose 22 concept words such as honesty, peace, and responsibility. Other schools may choose other words. They focus on them for a month at a time over a two-year cycle (no August). The words are introduced in school assemblies, used in the classroom, and drawn into playground disputes or situations in the dining room or around the school. Simply, the positive concepts are everywhere throughout the school day, and then beyond.

The words and the fullness of their meanings are examined in different ways. An essential feature is the practice of silent sitting, a special kind of reflection which is introduced to the very youngest children and done by all age groups not only during assemblies but intermittently throughout the day. It brings calm and concentration, and a means for each child to appreciate and comprehend her or his own, profound, inner self. Another important element is class discussion of behavioural dilemmas. This is undertaken dispassionately in the light of the positive words, and adult behaviour may also be questioned by children. These practices develop the ability to observe and consider actions and thus to notice what part one has played in situations, whether positive or negative.

After a period consolidating this work from within the Oxfordshire Education Authority, Neil Hawkes is working as an education consultant specialising in its practical application in different situations. He says, "Despite what happens in the external world, no-one can take away the freedom to choose our attitude, and values education enables the foundations for making this choice to be put in place. Children can reach the freedom to make choices by reflecting, thinking deeply, and creating understanding and then wisdom (called spiritual intelligence). No other part of the curriculum is concerned with the internal world of the child, and hence with developing this facility.

"Also, by developing values, we are filling the vacuum. If you ask people, 'what is it that matters in life?', most will answer in terms of meaning. Values helps to develop that. If we have no meaning based in religion or ethics, we are in a materialistic paradigm which simply creates boredom. Values education provides the antidote."

Of course, it is the crises in life that force such serious thinking upon us. For those without the basic tools to undertake this thinking, crisis is much harder to bear. Mr Hawkes says he often asks himself, "Am I being realistic? Can it help not to react instinctively?" The question can also be put, "To what extent does values help keep this instinctive, brute reaction in check?" The reply is that although no-one claims to have all the answers, the values work can help, and does help, in normal life.

This updated précis of the original Quiet Revolution also contains new material from values schools featured in the DfES report.

AT WEST KIDLINGTON

THE CHILDREN OF West Kidlington Primary School, in the county of Oxfordshire, in the south of England, are exceptionally lucky.

This is because values education was successfully pioneered there.

It teaches the children – and the adults who care for them – the skill of looking through a positive lens to a clear and steady view, uncluttered by negative expectation. This magical outlook stems from work that involves everyone in exciting aspiration.

It is said that when the expectation is high, the general standards are high. The positive values curriculum creates beautiful and powerful expectations. Thus it enables solutions. It sees not problems, but situations that can be solved.

Let's come out at this early stage about what it's really about, and put forward the prospect of spiritual transformation through this work.

To start with: the school. The school is the literal context, and the metaphor is the school of life. The school is a dramatic, microcosmic, self-contained world. For children, it is the foundation for the adult world. For adults, it is a multi-layered community, a setting for subtle and complex interactions. It is education in the largest sense: the expansion of understanding.

The dramatic locations are:

- the playground, with its friendships, disputes, and tests of strength and honour
- the classroom, where so much more is learned than simply examinable subject matter
- the head teacher's office, where problems and troubles are shared, and achievements celebrated
- the school hall, where the harmonious community is created through reflection and discussion.

A school community is like the community of a village or a small town, or the living and working community within a company, a shop, or a street. The questions, confusions and joys are the same. The effort is the same: to live and thrive and work and play and be content. The purpose is to do these things within the community in such a way that each individual child/adult succeeds within the group; and to discover how to be just as happy alone as in company.

Wonderfully, all this was made possible in Oxfordshire at the end of the last millennium. The profound work at West Kidlington Primary School transformed many lives, and continues to do so. It involves children, adults, teachers, parents, school administrators, kitchen staff and caretakers, and it influences the visitors from different parts of the country and from abroad, it also influences many of the people of the village of West Kidlington itself. This unassuming place is a few miles north of, and a world away from, the world-famous university city of Oxford. The population of West Kidlington merits town status, but quirkily defends the definition of village along with its independence from its illustrious neighbour.

A Quiet Revolution was written at the end of the seven year headship of Neil Hawkes, and was sold in 20 countries. Since publication, the progress that individuals, schools and groups have made is one of joyfulness. It comes from learning to value the best self and release its full creativity to flourish in the everyday world. Neil Hawkes recommends, "celebrating your qualities and dispositions, and enjoying *being*". Socially, the first question on meeting someone is often, "What do you do?" and they are assessed in that light. If we were more concerned to know in full, "*Who are you?*" we could make a different world. We don't ask children, "What do you do?" We take an interest in *who they are*.

The revolution, whether for children or adults, teaches us to ask, consciously or unconsciously:

Who am I when I like myself?

- and to recognise and respond to it. The children of West Kidlington Primary School understand that this question is the same as the next one:

Who am I when I am the best that I can be?

- and that it has the same answer. The children understand this without having to go to the trouble of articulating it, they know it in their bones. But for grown-ups, the frequent reiteration of this question is life-changing. It assumes that each of us knows and delights in our best self, and can free it to determine how we live. This creates an outlook that seeks possibility, choice and freedom. Neil Hawkes sums it up thus: "the key to it is finding the window to your own deeper magic, and opening it a bit wider".

Here is West Kidlington Primary School's positive value lexicon:

Quality	*Co-Operation*
Unity	*Understanding*
Peace	*Honesty*
Happiness	*Appreciation*
Hope	*Courage*
Patience	*Love*
Caring	*Friendship*
Humility	*Thoughtfulness*
Simplicity	*Tolerance*
Trust	*Responsibility*
Freedom	*Respect*

These essential concepts are explained in assemblies through stories and plays, and used throughout the school day: in the playground, in dedicated values lessons, simply whenever the camera lens of perception needs to be positively refocused. The daily practice of silent reflection always begins assembly, and is essential to the method. (Other schools doing this work choose their own value words, an important exercise.)

The work in this big village school of 400+ pupils shows how things can be when everyone tries their hardest within a simple, purposeful framework, and backs each other up as they go along. All of the children and the adults are concerned in investigating the values they live by. Incidentally, 12 of the words come into every such list made in any part of the world.

Deep understanding of the positive concepts gradually permeates the layers of individual consciousness by a kind of osmosis, and ultimately is internalised to the point where the concepts govern action without having to be consciously invoked. However, if you ask the children to say why they chose one course of action over another they often say, "I thought of my values" (NB possessive pronoun). During the preparation of *A Quiet Revolution* one little boy in explaining a situation to me said, "I didn't know whether I should be doing co-operation or respect, so I thought I'd try and do both".

For adults, the process may have to be more deliberate. We have mostly been brought up to determine our behaviour according to what will bring praise, or at any rate avoid trouble. In other words, to respond to external stimulus. Elevated decisions based on our inner excellence may be less familiar, although with practice we can get as good at it as the children are.

TALKING

THE NEXT PART of the method is the discussion of the words. The conversations focus on actions and results, and children consider problematic incidents with their classmates and teachers. They produce difficult questions unselfconsciously at such sessions and the teacher takes the opportunity to bring the focus back to the value concept word of the moment.

This exercise starts very early in the children's school lives. One Christmas at West Kidlington I watched five and six-year-olds discuss happiness. The first question, "What makes you happy?" was put to each child in turn. The answers were predictably simple. "I like it when I get a hug", "I like it when my mum reads me a story". The second question, "what do you do that makes people happy?" brought answers in the general area of, "my mum likes it when I tidy my room", and "my dad likes it when I say thank you".

It is the second question that is revolutionary, because in answering it, the children were beginning to see that they could create happiness in others. Over time, the corollary, that they are can just as easily do the opposite, would dawn upon them. We all have an effect. Every action has a result - as indeed does inaction. On that day, as on all other days, the children were sensitively shown how to consider other people's points of view and thus to observe their own part in the whole. In the course of their primary school life they will gradually see that they are in charge of - and therefore responsible for - their own destiny. As adults, our own part in our everyday dramas and in the larger dramas of the world stage becomes clearer as we make the same kind of excursion into our inner selves.

Thus the complex concepts and their deep implications are internalised and developed. How do the positive concepts affect behaviour, and what do they mean to the children's appreciation of themselves as excellent human beings? The effort in its entirety is how to achieve the greatest happiness for the greatest number. The children and the adults see how enjoyable it is when they get it right.

This apparently simple tale has great relevance in a world that is desperately short of unifying principles. The children of West Kidlington Primary School know who they are, and they know that they are valuable. Because of this they have no need to boast or show off, or push and shove, or take up anyone else's space, whether inner or outer. Their confidence is deeply and properly founded.

The children observe their thoughts and actions from a position of inner strength. They can do this because the adults who teach and care for them have great respect for them. The adults understand that they too are learning, and they teach and support the children while acknowledging that sometimes the children may be wiser than they are themselves. Thus the phenomenon is circular and not linear, all participate, and each is essential to the whole. It follows that all the grown-ups must value themselves too.

Eugene Symonds is now the head of West Kidlington Primary School, and, like Neil Hawkes, says he is still learning all the time. He speaks of the positive values method with something approaching wonder, especially in the matter of discipline. "I don't seem to have to say very much to the children now, they already know what's wanted," he explains. "If a child is sent to me I can usually say, 'can you remember what we talked about in assembly, and could you just go into the hall [where the value of the month is on display] and come back and tell me what the word is?' – and they'll go and look, and come back and say, 'I know what I should have done, I'm sorry' – and that's enough. It's amazing! I often get written apologies that I haven't asked for. It's all so clear. You only have to remind them."

All of the values school communities interpret the ideas slightly differently, but all of their lives are enhanced by them. They are differently situated and have different difficulties, different aspirations. But though the interpretations may vary slightly in the detail, the three main elements are always retained. They are these:

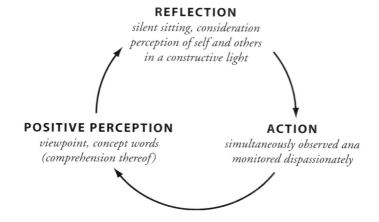

REFLECTION
*silent sitting, consideration
perception of self and others
in a constructive light*

ACTION
*simultaneously observed and
monitored dispassionately*

POSITIVE PERCEPTION
*viewpoint, concept words
(comprehension thereof)*

Here is how to have your own Quiet Revolution.

• First, see yourself positively. This is a delightful, and for many quite a novel exercise. You may need to constantly refocus your personal viewfinder to get the hang of it.

- This vision will enable you to see the world positively.

- Practising silent reflection every day is vital, in order to learn to observe oneself and the world dispassionately.

- Take considered action, and simultaneously monitor it.

- These activities go in a circle, each moving into the next. The totality might be called a Circle of Power.

In time, everyone who does these things becomes calmer, less easily upset by external events, more in command of themselves, and more in command of their position in the world. And, what a bonus – it all begins with a real appreciation of the self. We can start by acquiring the habit of congratulating ourselves when we notice that we've got something right.

Have a look at the way the little communities of children and adults work things out, try it yourself for a week, and the world will be a sunnier place. You find you are more wonderful than you knew. The magnificence inside you is being invited out, through the vision and encouragement of children around the world.

POSITIVE FOCUS

A DRAMATIC CHANGE of view: here is the cup half full, instead of the half empty kind.

The Quiet Revolutionary view begins with a positive focus. Once your viewpoint changes, it follows as day follows night that your feelings about yourself and your place in the world are transformed too. You see that you are valuable and purposeful, an essential part of the picture. This is as true for an adult as it is for a five-year-old.

This was my perception when I first went to West Kidlington Primary School and it has continued throughout my involvement with that fine establishment and the many others that have taken up the values work. Incidentally, my observations are those of an education journalist and children's writer, not a professional teacher.

The children and the adults in the school communities learned to see themselves as worthwhile. Of course, the self that is being observed at this point is the inner, essential being. This is the reverse of the ego-trip, it's genuine appreciation. From this position, everyone in the school communities can have the self confidence (confidence, from Latin, con – with; fido – trust/faith) to make big changes. Be content with who you are! That's the starting point.

The main elements of the Quiet Revolution look like this:

- Giving attention to the inner world of thoughts and feelings
- Reflection and consideration before action
- Adults as good listeners
- Adults as models for children
- The building of heart and soul, mind and body
- Emotional stability
- Sensitive listening
- Calm discussion
- Careful consideration of values decided by the school community

For teachers, there are classroom resources (*see* bibliography). The big Values Lessons folder developed at West Kidlington Primary School places the strongest emphasis on the behaviour of adults. The school ethos and the pervasive atmosphere are the most crucial influences on the children. Here, the old-fashioned phrase *setting an example* (known to teachers as modelling) comes back into play. We can't ask of children what we don't at least attempt to do ourselves. Honest, straightforward communication is the key. We may ask, is time set aside to listen to the views of pupils? How are visitors greeted?

The bedrock of all these efforts is the school assembly. This is where the tone is set, and the aspirations are articulated.

ASSEMBLY

ALL OF THE elements of values education are in place all day long - in lessons, in the playground, at school dinner time, walking around the corridors - and understanding them starts in assembly. At West Kidlington Primary School everyone enjoys assembly, and this in itself is revolutionary. How many people can say they enjoyed school assembly? Not so many.

Positive values assemblies are serious and important. They are not seen as just a chore to be got through. At West Kidlington, assemblies are held every day, all slightly different, but all serving a positive purpose and contributing to the cohesive harmony that makes the school so unusual. At the heart of the assemblies is an affirmation of the school's identity and a reinforcement of the strength of the community.

A great deal of effort goes into the planning and presentation of what look like simple meetings, in order to create the atmosphere of alert stillness, the correct conditions for calm concentration, to ensure the precise balance of content. Consistency of behaviour is exemplified by the teachers. In many school assemblies you see teachers talking while children are expected to be silent, this is not so at West Kidlington and demonstrates one of its great strengths: the personal commitment of all the adults to proper behaviour. Just as the teachers must not talk, so they must not arrive late. For the children, even the manner of walking into the assembly hall is critical: nudging and giggling and whispering are not seen.

Sue Booys is a Church of England vicar whose son attended the school. She said, "The attention to detail matters very much. It matters that, for example, the head teacher is always in assembly before it starts – in many places a busy head would consider that a waste of time". It is part of the ritual that whoever takes assembly must be sitting in the hall before the children begin to file silently in. They are accompanied by their class teachers, and they wait for a signal before seating themselves in rows.

The ceremonial nature of the beginning sets the tone and marks the boundaries, but instead of feeling restrictive, it creates security. There are no sulky or miserable faces. Though the children walk in silence they are not oppressed, they are already imbibing the spirit of the event. They are alert, ready to join in the meeting, focused upon it - and thus, focused upon the school and the day to come.

Ellen Gardner, parent and school helper, remarked on the mood of it. "I notice that no-one drags their feet when they're walking in to assembly. They stand nice and straight, their heads high". Furthermore, "It's a different way of silence the children have there. They do their silence out of respect."

Monday. On the first day of the week the head teacher takes assembly for Key Stage 2 pupils (seven-11-year-olds). The month's value word is introduced. The week's word is in the spirit of the prescribed Acts of Worship for schools, and the additional theme words for each month have been chosen by the staff and are used throughout the curriculum. Year Three teacher Mrs Conroy expresses the staff room consensus on the first assembly of the week. "It's essential for the staff as well as the children. You have to bring your attention back to school, you need to focus on school and duty and the children, and the Monday assembly pulls all that together. I enjoy it, but I need it too. I think it serves more purposes than you can really define." Weekends dissipate the working frame of mind, and in a community that works in groups, the restoration of purposeful concentration to each individual participant influences the total effort.

The children file in class by class with their teachers and sit down on the wooden floor of their pretty assembly hall. A great deal of effort has been put into creating a reflective atmosphere through lighting and music. The children's voices can be amplified if necessary; coloured spotlights create pools of light which concentrate attention on the centre of activity. The children have to be seated precisely by their teachers for there to be enough room. Occasionally some of them need to be shifted slightly to accommodate others; this is done without fuss. Light comes through huge skylights and from the side corridor into a room that is simple and uncluttered. The children's faces are concentrated, and the convention of silence is long-established. Pleasant, calming music plays on a tape. The head teacher sits in the state of stillness that he wishes the children to have, silently acknowledging each child but focussed within himself.

When everyone is in place, the head teacher stands up and starts the assembly. This one was given by Neil Hawkes one Monday in June.

"Welcome! I hope you used the weekend to do things... I did a lot of things, lots of them were good fun, some were relaxing and some were chores, and this morning I was out in the garden early, looking at my pond, which is a favourite place in my garden. I saw it first with raindrops falling on it, they were bouncing on the surface, then when the rain stopped I saw it when it was quite still. Then a dragonfly landed on it and that brought a surface change, little ripples moved outwards from where this very beautiful insect had been. The surface of a pond is like our thoughts: sometimes jangly, sometimes peaceful. We need to make our minds relaxed but alert, so we can deal with our problems without upsetting ourselves."

Thus the week begins, with a greeting to everyone, a brief reference to weekend activities, and a visual story with a calming purpose. The transition between home and school, play and work is set in motion. A song is announced, the positive, jolly, life-affirming sort, vaguely but not always overtly religious. The projector that puts the words onto the wall is operated by children; the music is played on the piano by a member of staff, or it may be recorded. Staff and children all join in. Many of them know the words by heart since they run through the songs in whole-school choir practice every Wednesday, and everyone seems to enjoy the singing. The song is not of the Victorian hymn book style but neither is it sugar-coated: again the proper balance is struck. To start the week when they were focussing on co-operation between countries they sang "World in Union". Alternatively there might be, "The sun has got his hat on!" or "The wise man built his house upon the rocks". A favourite with the younger children goes, "If I were - " this or that animal, a *butterfly* perhaps, or a *busy, busy bee,* and each verse has the rousing chorus "but I just thank you Lord for making me *me*!"

Next there is likely to be a story, often practical and homespun, possibly describing something that happened over the weekend, possibly a simple story from the Bible or other sacred text. The story gives rise to contemplative thought. It will link into the theme and lead to another more general thought, there may be a moment of silence focussing upon the current word, and then there is whole school reflection. All this applies to the very young children too. (In assemblies for younger pupils the story often involves drama - "who would like to come out and play Joseph's wife?" or joining hands, or looking in a certain direction - and there is always a demand for concentration and understanding.) The final request is silent sitting for reflection.

REFLECTION

This morning in a moment of silence let us sit very still, close our eyes and feel relaxed. See yourself in your classroom, working hard at an activity, co-operating with others. Feel good about this work. Now think about our month's value - the value of trust - and think about someone you really trust. How do we become trustworthy, so others will trust us? What qualities do we need to develop? Patience, tact, friendliness, co-operation, honesty, may be some of the qualities. Choose one to think about during the day....Now open your eyes again.

The practice of reflection is at least as rare in schools as it is in the larger world. Here it is led, focused; it is the beginning of the school day, in this instance the beginning of the school week. It brings the children back to focus upon the positive aspects of themselves that they can value. In a world that talks of low self-esteem yet so often seems to reinforce it, here is the antidote. It is almost immeasurably useful to bring each child back to their central worth, to the parts of themselves of which they can feel most proud. This practice builds the faith in the self that knows it can return to the place of inner excellence and find the strength for making changes when necessary.

In academic terms, educationalists who are concerned about a perceived trend towards short-term concentration look with wonder upon children who can not only sustain a school assembly of 20-25 minutes without talking or giggling, but also focus on it, maintain the idea, and finally remain for several minutes in silent contemplation of a positive concept. The effect of this daily concentration exercise on the mental capabilities would be beneficial by itself. The effect of the calming and stilling of the emotions is an addition of great worth.

The meeting is closed with a prayer, the music goes back on, and the orderly processions begin again. There is total calm. It takes several minutes for the children to leave the hall, while the head teacher sits at the front, not moving, not talking, but contemplative. Once again he takes the opportunity of making eye contact with individual children. The teachers who brought their rows of children into the room signal to the children to rise in the order they came in, and in that order they leave. Those who are waiting to go, wait in silence.

It is almost impossible to imagine that this event, and variations on it, takes place daily without coercion or misbehaviour at West Kidlington and many of the schools that have taken up the positive values method. That is because bad behaviour is so often the norm elsewhere. The positive focus ensures that the effect of this Monday assembly is to bring the whole school back together again, to concentrate upon the week ahead, on its objectives and the tools that will be used to achieve them. What is being demonstrated is a remarkable synthesis of the reiteration of the value of each individual child and their individual thoughts and abilities, reiteration of the importance of those elements to the community, reiteration of the secure place of each child within the school, and finally, at a subtle but powerful level, a reminder of the importance of the school itself. A very complex web of ideas, observations and intentions is being woven. The children are invited to consider their inner capabilities, their positive worth, their place in the community and their purpose for the week, and to do it from the touchstone of that month's positive concept. They answer in the affirmative, and then they are focused, positive, calm, and ready to start. And as it was established more than a decade ago, so it is now.

Pupils say they enjoy assemblies at West Kidlington and miss them when they leave. This is in contrast with a generally negative feeling among the general public for assemblies or meetings, which paradoxically accompanies a wringing of hands over the dissipation of many of the traditional frameworks for providing individual security and defining social behaviour. Meanwhile the phenomenon of social fragmentation manifests not only as personal distress for many, but also as confusion about where we belong, and who are our neighbours.

But though we may have little enthusiasm for assembling, we will admit to missing our context: the village-style community, the long-established support networks, the sense of belonging. Hence therapy groups and television soaps. Many social mechanisms such as church-going or membership of local societies are also declining. Without a core, whether of family, industry, activity, belief system or a mix of all of them, society and social life are confused and fragmented. However this marvellous opportunity for re-creating at least some part of it exists in every school, and it is in the school assembly.

Here, each member of the community is invited to find their personal worth, and the common purpose, and to see themselves as part of the whole. These are not new ideas. It is the manner of presenting them, and the consistency of perception within the positive values school communities that is revolutionary. The emphasis on individual responsibility that applies right down to the five-year-olds

is nothing short of extraordinary. For many years, attempts to weld
school communities together was based on edicts from above, backed
by systems of punishment. By contrast, this method starts from the
value of each individual child and allows them to see their part in their
world. "If I do this, how will it affect me - and how will it affect the
others?" In teaching this self-questioning, adults must become
personally involved in it. The understanding is begun in assembly.

The teachers find the spiritual exercises invaluable. When they
take the assemblies they must work within local authority agreed
guidelines and maintain the ethical position of the school. They do so
with great aplomb and some differences of style, and they say that it
not only teaches them a great deal but also touches them inwardly.
The *manner* of the assembly is critically important. The original head
teacher's notes made for guidance of the staff who wished to take
assemblies included these:

"Our Assemblies, which include our Acts of Worship [the legal
obligation], are one of the main ways by which we create our positive
reflective ethos. All colleagues make a tremendous contribution
through their presence and active participation. Pupils are very aware
that all staff, by their positive attitude, involve themselves in
assemblies, acting as role models for them to emulate... Assemblies
should contain times of quiet reflection which enable pupils to
develop the deepest values and aspirations of the human spirit (eg
love, peace, wonder, imagination, sensitivity and integrity)... Silent
reflection is a key element. It is especially important to remind pupils
about expected behaviour when coming to and returning from the
Hall from across the playground."

Tuesday. The juniors had the assembly hall to themselves and the
younger children went to assemblies in their own classrooms. This

junior assembly was taken by Karen Errington, who later took up the deputy headship of Windmill Primary School, in the city of Oxford.

Here it is..

It takes nearly five minutes for all the children to come into the hall. They sit in their orderly rows, some of them turn round to look at each other, perhaps even smile a little, but as always they don't talk. The song is, "Hushabye Mountain". It is nearly the end of the summer term, so when the teacher asks the children to close their eyes and then says, "if you were packing a suitcase.." some minds dart to the holidays. But the sentence continues "...for a *baby*," and asks a big question, "what would you put in for the whole of its life on earth?" Karen Errington asks the children to open their eyes and give their suggestions.

"Toys." "Teddy." "Loving care." "Clothes." "Good health." "Money." "Education." "Friends," they say.

Next there's a Bible story about a farmer who had too much grain and began to build a bigger barn to store it in rather than give the surplus away, but died in the night before he could enjoy his anticipated riches. Foolish farmer!

"How do you feel when you give a present?" asks Miss Errington.

"I like the expression on their face!" says a girl, "makes me feel warm," says a boy, "you can feel a bit shy," confides a girl. The general opinion is that giving a present makes you feel very good.

The assembly continues, and after about quarter of an hour there is some minor shuffling, but still no talking. Three children read short poems, then the teacher takes the meeting back into her own hands. The final message is this: "Close your eyes and think about the richness in your life, the things you can't buy. A special memory, a hug from someone special, chatting with someone special, knowing you are loved. Just one special thing." Silence. Music. It's over. Then the orderly, silent departure.

Karen Errington was delighted by the response to the baby's suitcase question. "I'd expected more material things," she said, "I thought I'd have to lead them to the more abstract ones, like love and health and friends. I think it shows they've taken in a lot this term. Hope so!"

She was glad that she had taken the opportunity to lead assemblies, and had learned much from watching other people's. "I've been in schools where assembly would just be a painful experience of crowd control", she said. "Here, they're much more focused. Using reflection asks the children to bring their own experiences, and draw from them. Here, with all of us there's a continuity, a harmony of presentation."

Karen Errington was enthusiastic about taking the values emphasis into the next school. "I think it gives the children space to think about their behaviour and others' behaviour, space to air their views. Before I came I'd worked in four or five schools, and I'd never walked into an assembly where all the children are silent and focused, as they are here. The reason is that on the first day, the teachers talk about the experience to the infants, and the expectation that assembly shouldn't be a passive arrangement. The children are reminded to move quietly around the school and they're shown how to line up. They know what's expected and they just do it, it's amazing. When I got here I couldn't believe it. A lot of people comment on it."

The content had impressed her too. "We did an assembly last term on understanding, on the need to understand. The children said we all needed to understand – why some of them can't read, or swim, things like that – then it moved into bigger things, why some of the children's parents couldn't get on. A boy whose parents' marriage was breaking up said he wanted the subject talked about, but that he himself couldn't talk about it because it would make him cry. I can't imagine anywhere else where that would have been possible, this is the most extraordinarily supportive place. It's the whole child we're concerned with - literacy, numeracy, heart and soul. The thing is, an unhappy child is not going to learn."

SYMPATHY

HERE IS ANOTHER powerful element. The children are so sensitive to one another's needs that they feel secure in introducing to the school assembly subjects of great emotional distress. Apparently the children who talked about the marriage breakdown acknowledged that it must be terrible for the boy but suggested that if his parents would be happier living separately, and the boy would be able to see that, it might not be so bad after all. Then they offered him their sympathy. This is very grown-up stuff indeed, in keeping with the activities in the rest of the school. Teachers say the values work gives clarity of thought, and on this showing it appears that it gives the children the ability to think through even domestic catastrophe. It also enables them to put themselves in the position of their schoolmates, and to understand their troubles.

Karen Errington said, "The whole-school ethos, the values work, it all genuinely empowers. When the teachers were asked at one of our meetings, what makes an effective teacher, we all answered the more obvious skills, planning and so on, but the head said we must think about what we do, be aware of the part we play in the school. It's the same for the children. The children do the coffee money, for example, they bring round the birthday cards for people to sign, they organise the games during playtimes. It gives them responsibility. When they operate the switchboard at lunchtime it's not just pretend with someone standing over them. They play a part in the life of the school, their responsibility is within the school community, it's much more than just responsibility for neat book work." Such responsibility gives the children enormous self-respect, a key to future success.

Wednesday Some of the West Kidlington assemblies were taken by people from outside the school, and occasionally someone let them down. Then the head teacher stepped in. On this occasion Neil Hawkes had to take an infant assembly with nothing prepared, and not only had the promised assembly leader not turned up, so neither had the pianist. As the clock moved up to nine, action had to be taken.

"Oh well," he said wryly, "here goes!"

And he set off to fix up the music and sit contemplatively in the hall…

It is a smaller group than usual and composed entirely of the youngest children, who come in and sit down as usual without speaking, placing themselves in the more intimate arrangement of a semi-circle. The head congratulates them on coming in quietly and announces that they will sing, "Come let us remember the joys of the town". Miraculously, Mrs Conroy from year three volunteers herself for the piano.

"Thank you *very much* Mrs Conroy!" says Mr Hawkes, visibly relieved. Mrs Conroy leads the singing with great gusto.

Mr Hawkes takes on a Bible story. ("Does anyone know what a Bible is? See if you can find a Bible in your home.") It's the story of Naman.

"Naman was a soldier, big and strong, fair, a good man, he *co-operated* with people." (This month, co-operation is the value word.)

A small boy is selected from several volunteers to come out and take the part of Naman. "But Naman has a secret illness. It's a skin problem, one we don't get here. It's called lep-ro-sy." The disease is explained as one that people were frightened of long ago in Biblical times but that is not a problem any more, and the story moves on. Naman goes to see the prophet Elisha, is told to wash in the river, "not once but seven times - we don't wash ourselves seven times when we have a bath, do we, but that's what Naman had to do!" Naman is miraculously cured.

By this time children represent all the characters in the tale. When the cure is made, Naman and his wife hold hands. "Then Naman went home and told everyone about it. You must trust and love God, that's what Naman said, and that's what we must do." There's a prayer of thanks, and a wish that the world would be a happy place, then a birthday announcement - it's Isaac's seventh and he speaks enthusiastically of a trip to the burger bar with his friends. It is all lovely.

However, there is another thing to say. There has been a minor stone-throwing incident. In general the positive medium of the assembly is not used for disciplinary matters, but after a moment's hesitation, Mr Hawkes has decided to mention this one. The incident is explained.

"When stones are thrown they always hurt something. So what would I want you to do with stones?"

"Not pick them up," says a boy.

"Yes!" says the head. "Put your hands up if you understand."

They are ready to conclude. Dolphin music is put on the tape, and the children file quietly out. For a meeting that started on a wing and a prayer, it went very well.

There was a sequel to this assembly when the elderly neighbours whose glass had suffered were invited in, "to see another side of us". It was Harvest Festival, and a beautiful occasion. The school community was packed into the hall, with the visitors seated at the back. A huge table was laden with fruit and vegetables and tins of food. Gentle music was played on the piano. Neil Hawkes welcomed the visitors and the assembly followed its course of story and song, including reference to the lack of food in some countries. The infants sang, "See the farmer sow the seed, Up the fields and down", and then it was over. "Let us give thanks now to God, in nature revealed," said Mr Hawkes, "and for this fine display. Keep your wonderful patience going while you're going out!"

The elder visitors said they found it all "touching" and "moving". They were amazed at the concentration, they applauded the content of the assembly, and said they loved living near the school and missed the children during the school holidays. On the matter of the stones, they were remarkably sympathetic.

"It was nothing really," said one. "We've all got grandchildren, we know these things can happen. The mistake was in laying a gravel path in the first place, children are bound to pick up bits of it. Boys will, anyhow." The others agreed that the incident had been well handled and the harm had been little and understandable.

These two assemblies demonstrate the ethic in the school. The first acknowledged a social and moral mistake; the second made restitution for it (the breakages had of course been paid for from the school fund). A lesson had been learned without damage to the children's self worth, and the circle completed by proper care of the neighbours. Provision was made for the well-being of the smaller and wider community, for singular and plural, the wishes of individuals and those of the group.

On *Thursdays* there were birthday assemblies, when all the infants whose birthday fell during that week were given birthday cards. They would all step out of their lines and receive their cards, and birthday stickers, and at the end of that summer term great patience was demanded of the assembled children because Sean, Rebecca, Lauren, Gemma, Chloe, Elise, Emma, Daniel, Jordan, Natasha, Matthew, Lindsay, Lewis, Charlotte, Kirsty, Kayley, Hayley, Ben, Lewis, Laurence, Tom, Philippa, Lee, and Aran, all had their birthdays at the end of term or in prospect in the holidays, and all were greeted and congratulated.

"Well done for the patient way we're doing this," said Neil Hawkes. The preferred method is always to praise excellence. Finally they all got to sing their birthday song, not *Happy Birthday*, but one with the chorus,

> *Strong to do right,*
> *Slow to do wrong,*
> *And thoughtful for others,*
> *All the day long.*

On *Fridays* the children did their own assemblies. These were rehearsed with the teachers but from year three (seven years old) onwards, performed by the children independently. This was very popular with the children during their time at the school, and remembered with pleasure when they left. It followed the pattern of song, play and poems, omitting only the reflection.

The year threes (aged seven and eight) who gave us an assembly on the theme of *co-operation* brought a playlet of a three-legged race which went very badly until a child urged the participants to co-operate, whereupon they set off running together instead of pulling against each other. First, the word *co-operation* was spelled out in the

American manner. "Gimme a *C!*" cried the first child in the line, the others shouted "*C!*" and the child held up a large paper C. "Gimme an *O!*" cried the next, "*O*" they cried - and so on.

Often the value words fit together. A class assembly given to the school on the subject of unity echoed the one on co-operation. It began after a delay of about five minutes caused by a teacher who wanted to record the event having difficulty with the video camera. The children sat silently and patiently waiting to start, and one of the teachers remarked later that she only realised how amazing it had been a week later when she recalled her other schools, "We'd have been hauling them out to the front, shouting at them, there'd have been talking and laughing. You don't realise how different it is here, it's another world."

At last the camera was fixed and the signal given for the children to start the assembly. Two of them stood at the front of the hall.

"Good morning!" said child one, "have you ever been lonely?"

"Sometimes it might be your own fault!" said child two.

"Here are two stories," said child one.

"The first one is: 'The Bee Who Wanted To Be Different'," announced child two.

There followed two playlets. In the first, a group of children dressed as bees applied themselves to the job of making a honeycomb from hexagonal pieces of paper representing the cells. However, one bee wanted to cut her paper in a different shape.

"I don't want to make six-sided cells!" she said wilfully.

"You can't do it like that!" said a co-operating bee.

"You'll have to take that cell out," said the child playing the teacher bee, "and make it the other way."

"No!" said wilful bee. The irregular cell could not be fitted into the honeycomb and she had to leave the hive, to her immense surprise and sorrow.

"When people or creatures want to live together, they must fit in," observed the commentator.

In story two, the population of a village attended four different churches, and the members of the congregations didn't speak to each other. A new family arrived, whose members divided themselves between the denominations. The villagers could not decide which of them to talk to. Then a terrible storm (excellent sound effects from the seated children) damaged the roof of the chapel. There was nothing for it but for all the villagers to help mend the roof, which they did, and departed shaking hands.

Mr Hawkes came to the front, congratulated the children, and spoke up for the oddball bee. "I think they probably let her back in," he said. There were useful remarks on the subject of doing things as a joint effort and doing them individually, with a recommendation for understanding. Unity had been shown simultaneously to mean fitting the pattern and accepting differences for the sake of happy co-existence, a fine paradox. Next, the children of the School Council gave certificates to various schoolmates to reward excellence: a caring attitude, helpfulness, smiling a lot. Each certificate-holder was congratulated by Mr Hawkes, who endorsed the positive qualities.

At the end of assemblies the children are invited to give notices or announcements and usually several give information in turn. They may announce a local or school event, or a fund-raising activity. They simply get up from their row, walk to the front of the hall, make their announcement clearly, go back to their place and sit down again, without fuss or organisation from adults. The head teacher saw this practice increasing. "Nowadays, more children are giving these notices than adults. And it isn't just the extroverts doing it, some of the shyest children do it too.

"The way they feel confident enough to get up and talk somehow says something about the way they see this as a school for all of us. They also know if they say something it has to be something of quality, they don't just get up for the sake of talking. The intensity with which the children listen to other children is extraordinary and very pleasing, and I'm sure it's partly because the adults also are exemplifying great joy - and really listening to the children. The children sense it and it gives them courage."

It happened that an academic observer from the USA was at this children's assembly.

"What's wonderful about all this," he said, "is the way the children are running their own, whole-school ethos, they're taking responsibility for it themselves. Also the way the School Council runs the community means they take responsibility for it." He is not the first to remark on the consistency of outlook, and the level of responsibility taken by the children. The way in which the children conduct their own assemblies is harmonious with the way they run the office at lunchtime. They are shown how to do it and entrusted with doing it properly. The result in both cases is a professional job. The children's assemblies are run by the children. The teachers bring their classes along to the hall, but no-one starts off the proceedings except the children, no-one operates equipment except the children: the event is their own. The confidence this gives them in their own presentation skills is another plus.

At the end of that summer term Mrs Conroy held several class assemblies on the subject of *journeys*, with particular reference to the following school year. Here the class assembly was being used, as quite often, to help towards an understanding of life changes. Her class was going up from what was infants to juniors (now known as year two to year three), and they were writing and talking about it and recalling their year in her class. Thus journeys began in class assembly and continued into class work. The children had brought pictures of themselves as babies and stuck them on the board, and they were trying to guess which of the babies had become whom in the class. Some of them read their essays anticipating life in the next year group. "I will be happy to be in Miss Pack's class and I will be sad to leave Mrs Conroy's class," wrote one of the girls.

They had written about the journey from seven to eight years old. "When I was in year two I could not do tens and units. My handwriting was appalling, now it's good," said one child. "I couldn't do my tables, didn't join up my letters," said another. Seven-year-old April had written a letter to the next class teacher. It had a border decorated with pictures of herself and the legend: "*I'm excited*". She gave herself a glowing reference. "In my report it said a lot of nice things like April is a delightful member of the class so I hope I am a delightful member of the class for you." However, there was a caveat. "But can I ask you a question do you give the children hard work? But when you try to answer that question I would like you to be **OHNEST** (sic)." A value word in context.

Mrs Conroy spoke of her own life journey, which had reached a crossroads the preceding Easter when she got married. The transitions in her life were related to the way in which the children were moving up the school.

"You find that you open up about yourself here, much more than usual," she said later. She believed that more required of the teachers, but that the experience was enriching. "My whole class and most of the school choir came to my wedding, and all their parents did too! It's very giving - and you have to give a lot in return. It's very equal, the expectations are very equal. Because I give a lot, they give a lot." Furthermore, "It's a big family, this school. My class, we see ourselves as a family within the community. It brings responsibilities."

Neil Hawkes saw the phenomenon of teachers taking assemblies as showing the success of informality within the structure. "Because we have a similar philosophy we pick up intuitively what each other is doing - and we can fill gaps swiftly if they appear," he said. He acknowledged his part in the transformation of the school assembly into a kind of meeting that welds the parts together. "Assemblies are the main vehicle for me to have a major influence on the school," he said, "I can influence them, staff as well as children, through the assembly. The big role of the head teacher is to be a leader, and the big quality is to be definite. There should be no ambiguity."

Thus the style of the positive values assemblies developed at West Kidlington sets the tone, defines and exemplifies the ethos, and is both prescriptive and descriptive. The way in which they are run demonstrates the policy of staff participation and the high level of democracy that applies to staff and children. The manner of them is quite formal. The way the pupils walk into the assembly hall is disciplined, yet they are not oppressed. The messages are clear and definite; the ethos is benevolent. Form and content demonstrate a wonderful synthesis of traditional and innovative thinking.

"Our assemblies create the climate for everyone to reach their inner space," said Neil Hawkes. "The traditional school assembly actively stops children from getting to that point within themselves." The tone of the school is set in assembly, and permeates the curriculum. West Kidlington Primary School sees it as the cornerstone of its efforts. The Reverend Sue Booys said, "the most important thing is wholeness. A whole community. This is not a place that is only devoted to teaching children *things*. The function of the school is that the children learn their academic stuff more effectively because they learn in a valued, structured environment. The quality of learning is better, and life skills and values are absorbed in ways they are in few other schools. No detail about people, individuals, or the conduct of the school, is considered unimportant. There's a clear sense of vision."

Similar thinking about the school assembly has influenced the other schools that have embarked upon their own individual Quiet Revolutions. There are differences of manner, but the commitment to harmonising the aspirations of the school communities is the same. The focus is positive, the message is positive, and if they go in for silent reflection, those few minutes are positive too. Silent reflection can of course be made available at other times than assembly, and at least one school has set up a Quiet Corner where children can go if they need to be calm and think things through. This place is a special kind of sanctuary.

Some values schools practise silent reflection at the beginning of every lesson, and they report that the children like it so much that they soon begin to ask for it spontaneously. It is most often used after sports or gym lessons, to calm things down. The assemblies vary somewhat from school to school, although most of them tend to avoid the old-fashioned discipline notices at the end. The objective is calm and harmony and the emphasis is on unity.

Differences can be created simply by timing. Afternoon assemblies are inevitably different. Beenham Primary School in Berkshire holds a Friday afternoon assembly for the upper age groups (eight to 11). Like West Kidlington, the assembly places emphasis on the current positive concept and includes a few minutes of silent reflection at the end, but at the conclusion of the school week the children are brought to a calm and clear departure for the weekend, with the events of the week put in perspective. It is a feeling of completion from which the participants can move calmly into the next stage of their lives. By establishing the practice of discarding aspects of the week that are dealt with and forming clear resolutions about matters still in hand, this can help to establish the invaluable skill of appraisal.

Within all of these serious efforts there are many opportunities for laughter. John Hulett, head of Barley Hill School in Thame, Oxfordshire, told me of an assembly at which he introduced the word Courage. Just to be provocative, he asked the school what their response would be if he told them to get up on the roof and then jump off it. The school assembly was agreed that the answer would be no. "Why?" asked Mr Hulett. He took the answer from a six year old girl at the front of the hall. "Because you didn't say 'please'," she said.

Some of the positive values schools spend more assembly time on world affairs; some use a background track of music; there are varying levels of pupil participation. It is the emphasis on the positive focus, on an outlook of possibility based within the strong inner self, that is the consistent feature. The practice of stopping all activity and giving time to be still for two or three minutes several times a day is also invaluable. The members of these school communities consider how they are feeling and whether they want to feel different. As a result of the practice of reflection, they discover that there really is a choice.

All of this effort works towards establishing school communities of balanced, emotionally stable, fulfilled, capable children and adults living purposeful lives in harmony together. They reach this highly desirable situation from a profound understanding and appreciation of themselves. It is the appreciation of their whole selves - not just the outer casing, but the essential excellence.

SPIRITUALITY

SPIRITUALITY CAN BE defined as the inner world of thoughts and feelings, carefully observed so as to lay the groundwork for the ultimate goal: aspiration or wish for transcendence. It was remarked that this quality is inherent within us all. However, although the need for it is inherent and must find nourishment, spirituality also needs to be worked on. The assemblies provide the context. The practices of observation and reflective stillness, and the habit of considering all sides of a question, build the ability to view the outer world dispassionately. From this viewpoint it can be engaged with in a more powerful way.

The Kidlington blueprint for values education provides children with mechanisms and vocabulary for gaining emotional intelligence. The school population talk about their feelings sometimes almost dispassionately. The constant exercising of the mind and perception within this framework refines the children's and the adults' own ability to use their inherent spirituality in their own ways. Another important feature of the Revolution is its democratising effect. Democratising and also revolutionary, because the concept of spirituality has until quite recently not been one that was spoken out loud.

The Quiet Revolution was the result of many influences coming together at an ideal moment. Everyone said that West Kidlington

Primary School had always been a happy place. Neil Hawkes went there when he had already had a considerable career in education and was viewing with disquiet the state of the nation vis à vis religious or moral understanding. He was concerned that no-one was setting any boundaries, and children were left floundering. He thought it was crazy to look for moral guidelines to arbitrary influences such as television, but he saw no-one taking up the challenge of showing children how to conduct themselves. He remarked:

"Children have to learn how to be in the world, how to deal with complex situations, how to observe and respond, and it is essential for them to do this from a position of strength and self-respect."

"The strength of the individual is inherent but needs to be nurtured."

"Efforts made on behalf of the positive, inner self are of enormous benefit to all the manifestations of the whole, visible person, including the understanding of academic subjects."

"The calm created by the habit of reflection brings to the learner a capacity for observation unfettered by the habits of worry or mind-flitting. In this way, a strong capacity for detached concentration is developed."

Neil Hawkes said that most educational theory made a serious omission. "It seemed that all the focus was on programming, and not on the condition and vision of the child. By this I mean, the *who* of the child. Most educational theorists look at what, how and where – not who. In education the answer to the question 'Who does it?' is the teacher, and to 'Who receives it?' the answer is the child. We don't tend to ask about the essential who of the child. 'Who is this person? What do they bring?' I like to think of the vision potential of the child as a human being and help them develop it. Consideration of the character, emotions and outlook, of the ability to make choices, the ability to acquire the information to make the choices, has been absent.

"You could say the heart was not being attended to. All was external, and the focus on educating the head alone left out heart and soul to the detriment of the whole human being. My concern was also to counterbalance the prevailing idea of happiness coming only from possessions and material success, and all the concentration on the external, with the capacity of each child to discover or perhaps rediscover their inherent harmony and comprehension." The phrase, 'the child as reflective learner' sums this up. It is the antithesis of programming. At its best, it reaches towards true independence of mind and action. When this is combined with harmonious participation in the community, and a clear sense of social responsibility, the goal has been reached."

CLASSWORK

REFLECTION IS USED not only during assemblies but also at the beginning of some of the lessons.

Reflection (Stilling/silent sitting)

Most of the lessons would have begun with a period of reflection. This is a time when the children are expected to sit still and silent for anything from one to four minutes, usually with some soft music and perhaps facilitating words from the teacher. It has proved to help children in a variety of ways. It regulates breath and heartbeat and so calms and relaxes the body. It quietens the mind, focuses attention and increases concentration. It helps to develop awareness and intuition, and the children are more able to get in touch with their own feelings.

This important practice also makes way for the value words to sink in, so that they are absorbed into the unconscious minds of the children for use when needed.

The positive lexicon is used in the school day as often as possible and it affects class work in different ways. A few lessons each week are dedicated to investigating the words. They must first be carefully defined, and there are exercises with which to do it. Some of these can be used for different age groups: the idea that Simplicity, for example, can be understood on a Spring walk, is offered for Year 5 (10-year-olds) as well as Year 1 (five-year-olds). The teachers' notes suggest looking at how beautiful things are in the natural world, talking about simple things such as landscapes, flowers, creatures, and activities such as dancing and singing. Two West Kidlington 10-year-olds define simplicity:

Joseph It's beautiful! Simplicity is beautiful. It means staying in the present, economy, using resources wisely, not wasting things, not being careless, giving time to your friends. I've missed some out but that's what I think it means.

Lucy We've been shown how simplicity is, how we can live better lives. Small things can make a difference. Like, if you did something for a person, even if it was somebody you didn't know, it changes things.

These children were helping to prepare an assembly for their class to give to the school. When the time came they defined simplicity as:

- natural (computer games vs. family meal)
- being natural (inner beauty: kind, loyal, trustworthy, loving)
- beautiful (animals, flowers, music)
- relaxing (daydreaming)
- staying in the present (neither reminiscing nor projecting)
- economy (no need for excessive material possessions such as too many clothes)
- giving friendship (patience, time), and
- appreciating even small things (a smile).

Five-year-old Joe said it was his favourite value word, and quietly gave a wonderful explanation of it. "Simplicity! I like simplicity. It's very calm. Motionless."

Within the small amount of discretionary time allowed within the time-table, an hour is taken every week at West Kidlington for each year group to chew over moral dilemmas. They do this with their class teacher, who is as far as possible impartial. During these lessons the children look at events in their lives, at whether something they did was in keeping with the positive concepts and their conscience, or perhaps how they might have done things differently. This exercise in self-awareness may be unique. It starts with considering what the words might mean, and it starts with the very young children. Values even come into the five and six year olds' circle time conversations. As the children progress up the school, the conversations naturally become more complex.

We joined Mrs Ball's year twos (aged around six), who had returned to their classroom from a lunch hour that had been too wet for them to play outside. Though they were feeling cooped up, they still had to sit quietly and hold their conversation. This formal task places quite a demand on young children. First, they sang the register, a charming introduction to the afternoon's work. Mrs Ball sang, "Jasmine, are you here?" Jasmine sang back, "Yes, Mrs Ball, I am here!" - and so on. It was the beginning of the spring term and there was a brief recollection of the value that ran up to the Christmas holidays, which was happiness.

The class opened with some memories of Christmas happiness, then moved to the January word, which was hope. Mrs Ball combined the concepts. "My hope at Christmas was that everybody would have a happy time," she said. "I wondered about an old man down the lane who lives alone but was ill in hospital." Next, she started on a box of objects she had prepared as conversation pieces for the topic. "In my box I've got things to show you. I'm going to ask you what you think I was hoping for at the times when I was using the objects." The first one was a black and white picture: an ultrasound scan of her daughter. "When I saw that picture, what do you think I was hoping for?" she asked.

"A girl?"

"No, it didn't matter."

"A baby!"

"Yes, I wished for a healthy baby, and that it would go very well."

A medal came out of the box. It belonged to Mr Ball's grandfather, who fought in the Second World War. He sent it home to his wife, who kept it close to her.

"What was she hoping for?"

"That he wouldn't be hurt," says a girl.

There were many more objects and photographs, many more comments, the children putting their hands up to speak and on the few occasions of children interrupting, being gently asked to wait for each other. The teacher summed up. Lastly there was a picture of a little Indian girl. The children said she looked poor, lonely and sad. Why? They thought she may not have enough food or water. A boy said the picture made it look as though the girl's parents didn't take enough care of her. Mrs Ball explained that this eight-year-old Indian girl supported her family, and her life was hard.

"What might she hope for, do you think?"

"Help."

"Something to eat."

The children concentrated well on this exercise despite the fact that they hadn't got out at lunchtime, which is especially troublesome for such a young group. There were two or three exits for the toilet, the teacher moved one or two children to sit close to her, but overall attention was held for nearly three-quarters of an hour. Lastly, each child was asked to say what they hoped for in the world.

Lee   I hope that everybody has a lovely home.

Jessica   I hope all children have food.

Francesca   I hope children get what they ask for.

Yasmin   I hope all children are OK, I hope they're safe.

Fava   I hope everybody stops fighting.

William   I hope everybody takes care of everybody.

"Yes," interjected Mrs Ball, "We're here, we imagine we're all brothers and sisters at school, but it's not like that everywhere is it? Let's have some more hopes, Andrew, what would you like people to be?"

"Healthy," said Andrew.

"Kind," said Lewis.

"Happy," said Kay.

"Everybody shares," said Ellis.

"There isn't a third world war," said Robin.

"Everybody has money, doesn't have to be poor," said Izzy.

"I hope in America they'll stop killing everybody because everybody's got guns," said Tracy.

"Everybody is kind," said Thomas.

"Mums and dads look after sisters and brothers," said Matthew.

"Well done, I think you've given good thoughts today!" said Mrs Ball, dispersing them to other tasks.

She was pleased with the class. "It worked pretty well," she said. "Something like hope is very abstract, I thought by bringing in something of my own, it would start the subject off. I was hoping for an understanding of someone else's life, what the other person might hope from it, and I think to an extent I got it.."

Social dynamics were noted.

"One of the most important things about a situation like this one is that the little ones learn that everyone's view is important. They must give each other time to answer. Then again, if they're off the point, you mustn't let them feel not valued. You have to bring the subject back without making them feel their opinion wasn't worth anything. Working in groups, co-operating, is still new. Who's on target, who finds it difficult, has got to be kept under constant review."

The progress of the subject matter had been, as so often, from the personal to the general. What happened in the Christmas holidays, how the neighbours fared, what were the hopes of the children for themselves and for the world: the conversations are directed from the smaller to the larger focus. "Who am I?" and "what is my place in the world?" are constant questions, as is, "how do my actions affect the community in which I find myself?"

Mrs Ball sees this as crucial. "Every day we talk about how we treat each other, how we treat the classroom. It's a constant concern that we must live and work together harmoniously. I have to explain this to parents, that how we are individually and as a group is so important."

Further up the school, the pupils had done written work on the same theme. Here are extracts from the writings of two of Linda Heppenstall's year fives (aged 10). Annie's is first.

"The things that make me happy are when I make other people happy by giving them presents or when I get love and care from my family and friends. I also get happy when I'm playing with other people.

"I can make other people happy by saying nice things to them, giving them presents, helping them, staying with someone if everyone else goes away. I can make my mum happy by doing what she says straight away."

This was illustrated with a picture of Annie (indicated with an arrow and the word *me*) offering a gift-wrapped box to another girl (marked *friend*) who was grinning hugely.

Such joyful altruism was no accident: the children had been asked to write first what made them happy, and then how they could make others happy. One boy said engagingly, "every second of the day I try really hard to make others happy". He expanded on this. "The things I do to make other people happy is to say nice things to everyone - and do nice things to them. Helping my mum with the housework make her very cherefull. When I clean my hamsters cage I know he is very happy because he has a spottlis tidy cage. He seems to have an insible simle [invisible smile]."

Linda Heppenstall's report on this exercise says:

"I was aware of the different levels of spiritual development in the class as the lesson proceeded. By the end I hoped the more able (ie more spiritually developed) would have grasped the idea of being able to control - to some extent - their level of happiness, by changing their thoughts and ways of looking at things - working towards an understanding that their happiness is their responsibility. I hoped the less able would identify the feeling of happiness and realise the less obvious things that help us to achieve it through giving, friendship, love (i.e. spiritual qualities within ourselves). My overall aim in these lessons is to help children realise how they can benefit themselves and others by developing these qualities within themselves.

"I felt a further discussion on the happiness scale would have been beneficial - about whether this is where we should seek to be or whether we should aim for a higher score - how possible or desirable would it be?"

ATMOSPHERE

EVERYDAY LIFE AT positive values schools has a particular grace which comes from the genuine care of members of the community for each another. The first time I visited Beenham, a small primary school in the Berkshire countryside, the head teacher's three year old daughter was in the school. She was too young to be a pupil there, but was poorly, and had to be brought to school for the day. The little girl was cared for by various members of staff and also by the children. They picked her up and carried her from room to room, played with her, talked to her, took her into the dining room for lunch: she was simply included in the community. Her security within this situation was obvious. She was no trouble at all, she went quite happily to whoever had the time and inclination to look after her — and there were plenty of volunteers. This level of consideration is typical of the ethos which is visible in the practical day-to-day life of these schools; you notice it as soon as you step through the door. The visitor waiting in Beenham's small hallway sees first the promotional school tea towel displayed on the wall. It is printed with children's drawings of the staff (stick people with big smiles, corkscrew hair, fingers like birds' feet). The imagination may play for a moment with the idea of going through the door into the school and finding that the staff really do look like that. Turning the gaze, the visitor sees an impressive number of silver cups for football and chess.

Beenham's dining room at lunchtime was a study in itself. The school had been giving attention to the quality and choice in the school dinners, and to the atmosphere in the dining room, with the result that many more children were choosing to have school dinners. Meals taken in the company of others are both a delight and a social demand. At the simplest level they form part of the training to be friendly and polite; in larger terms the sharing of food is profound and significant. Beenham's harmonising efforts, however were beginning to cause a different kind of headache for the head teacher: school meals were becoming so popular that they might be going to need two sittings. There was some apprehension that this could reduce the social coherence so happily built up. For the time being, however, it was working very well, and the children were animated and polite as they ate together.

Atmosphere tells a great deal. The harmony in the foyer of West Kidlington School is as tangible as the light that floods in through its glass roof. When you arrive, a child will stop to ask if you need directions, then go on their way. At reception they discover your purpose, set it in motion, and offer you a cup of tea. Your welcome is calm, purposeful and hospitable. West Kidlington children are polite and centred and because their confidence comes from within it does not take the form of showing off (although they do like to show you their work).

The children take on increasing levels of responsibility within the school community as they grow up, and the older children volunteer for everyday tasks, including running the office at lunchtime. This works extraordinarily well. The job includes not only answering the phone but also looking after visitors and occasionally directing workmen to the right building. Two children arrive at midday with their sandwiches, to be briefed by the office administrators.

"A man called Steve is laying a pipe for the new outside classroom and he's expecting a terribly important call. Will you make sure to find him and bring him to the phone when someone rings up and asks for him?"

"Yes, Mrs Lobban."

"You're sure you know which classroom I mean?"

"Yes."

"Good, excellent, and if you get a moment there's these leaflets to fold. They've been counted into class piles but I want them ready to distribute to all the classrooms. Good luck, girls, enjoy yourselves!"

The girls perform their tasks with panache.

"Good afternoon, West Kidlington School, how may I help?"

"Can I speak to Mrs Brennan please?"

"I think she's in the staff room, would you like me to go and see for you?" or perhaps, "She's not in school at the moment, she should be back after lunch, can I take a message?"

The children are helpful, polite and businesslike, they know where everyone is or where to look for them. They are careful not to leave the caller holding on without information. "I've just looked in the staff room and he isn't there but Mrs Chamberlain says he'll be back in 10 minutes, would you like to ring back or shall I take a message?"

The phone call for Steve comes about five minutes after Mrs Lobban's departure, and by lucky chance he is in the school foyer. One office child goes to bring him into the office while the other works out how to switch the call through to the extension. The lunchtime office staff also greet visitors, ask them politely to sign the visitors' book,

find out who they want to see, and offer to take them to the person
or find the person for them. Of all these tasks, the one they say they
like best is answering the phone.

Asked whether they had offered to do the lunchtime office shift
or were chosen, the children said they had been chosen. This turned
out to be only half the story. Actually, at that time many more
volunteered than were needed, and the teachers selected those they
thought were most likely to do the job well. It was certainly true that
these two got the office right: everything went like clockwork.

To begin with the phone rings about every two minutes, then for
a while not at all. They start to fold the leaflets, which are about the
Easter programme at the sports centre, where swimming sessions and
a Sporty Fun Club for eight to 13-year-olds are promised.

A girl comes by volunteering to do a job, but they have nothing
for her. "Plants?" she wonders. "'Fraid not," they say, "we've already
done them." She sighs and walks away. "I'll come back tomorrow," she
says. There is a truly astonishing amount of volunteering. At
12.40pm, two boys collect the class registers that were brought there
at midday, and take them back to the classrooms. Steve the electrician
gets another call and this time one of the girls has to go and find him,
and thus the co-ordination of the gas and electricity fitting to the new
auxiliary classroom can proceed towards completion on Friday, when
the room is needed for use.

At one o'clock the girls hand the office back to the administrative
staff, explain the business of their hour, everyone thanks everyone else,
and the children go off to their afternoon classes. They've had no time
to play but they have eaten their picnic lunches, performed the office
tasks, and sometimes done an extra job: operated the shredder,
perhaps, or helped with leaflets. They say they enjoy doing the extra
jobs very much. Sometimes they also fit in a bit of their own

homework. The children are especially assiduous at selling lapel pins or flowers for charity and the teachers say they often have to dodge them. Having greeted a visitor and directed them to where they want to go, the children may remember they have not done this crucial part of their job. One of them races madly out of the office in pursuit of the visitor's back. *"We're supposed to sell you a poppy!"* she cries.

Thus the ordinary and everyday provide constant opportunities for putting the concepts into practice. When the children of West Kidlington School run the office at lunchtime they really run the office, it's not just playing at it with an adult on hand to take over. They understand the responsibility and take pride in assuming it. There are always more volunteers for the office rota than are needed. The children are treated like capable people, and they rise to it. As they do the work, they demonstrate the values they have learned: they are considerate, sensitive and polite as they answer the phone or greet visitors. The positive outlook which grows out of the practices of reflection, perception, and observation of action, is not confined to special lessons or even to assembly. At best, its results are visible all the time. The inner security of each member of the community is shown in the way they deal with one another, the way they refer to old-fashioned virtues in determining their course of action. It is safe to do the right thing at West Kidlington, doing the right thing is seen to bring terrific personal and social rewards.

Schools in England and elsewhere have adapted the positive values method to their particular needs. They had different motives for doing so. Not least among these are the schools with many different faith traditions represented in the school populations, and those with a large proportion of children from families with no particular religious allegiance at all. Some schools that were in the middle of disruption found instant improvement, although in its fullness the method takes quite a long time to take root. One of the values schools in the west of England had experienced serious discipline problems. Another had been socially divided, no-one was really communicating with anyone, and the effect on the children's behaviour had been predictably disastrous.

What happens when they introduce the values method? Generally there is an instantly noticeable improvement. Of course, the method takes a while to become thoroughly embedded, and then has to be constantly observed and tweaked. There is variation in interpretation and understanding, but the many of the letters sent to its originator sound broadly like this:

"We started with Co-operation. I introduced it in an assembly to which every member of staff was invited. Teachers followed this value up in a class lesson and during circle time. Staff referred to it at every opportunity. It was amazing to listen to the very youngest children talking about co-operating with others. We used the Oxfordshire Values Education file as a resource, and soon made a collection of other books and pictures. Over the year we worked on 11 values. We had the value of Tolerance during July: we were very aware of how nerves can be strained at that time of year. The value of Peace went very well, and our outside playhouse was transformed into a PEACE ZONE. Over the period of Lent and Easter we looked carefully at the value of Hope. We collected school equipment for a school in the Gambia, and the children became very involved in thinking about others.

"I regularly informed the parents about our value of the month and gave them ideas of how to reinforce the value at home. The value of the month is prominently displayed throughout the school. We have now made a two-year plan in which 22 values are taught.

"The introduction of a school council linked well with our values, and the councillors select a child each week for an award. The child is chosen because he/she has demonstrated the value of the month. An unexpected result of the values education has been the level of involvement of our mealtime assistants. They have really taken it on board and their attitudes to the children have improved immensely. They also look out for children who have developed the value of the month and they have responsibility for awarding lunchtime certificates. They are part of the team.

"We had our OFSTED inspection in October, 2003. The team was very impressed with the values education. They talked with the children, who were able to discuss a wide range of values and explain what they were. The assemblies referred to the values, and the spiritual and moral development of the children was judged as very good. The inspectors judged that the involvement of the school dinner supervisors in the values education was a strength of the school. One of the team inspectors was so impressed that he has contacted the LEA to order a copy of the values education file!

"The team liked the way that the '*staff were held together by underpinning values*'. One inspector commented that the children were very lucky to come here. Praise indeed. What I liked best of all was a remark made by one of our 'special' year 2 boys. He met an inspector in the corridor and asked him, 'Who are you?' When he heard that he was an inspector he told him, 'This is a good school'. I'm pleased to say that they agreed."

Frances Taylor,
St Nicholas Infants School,
Wallingford, Oxfordshire

The values education report written by Dr Tony Eaude said that every school in the study had noticed instant improvement in relationships, whether between children and children, between adults and adults, or between children and adults. The schools were also unanimous on better manners, more co-operation and consideration. In many cases they reported better concentration, and for two of them, inspectors themselves attributed enhanced academic results to the sense of calm and emotional security they had seen in the schools. Dr Eaude's report was commissioned at an early point in the introduction of the method in just nine of the many schools that have taken it up. The result was encouraging, for the method was found to be useful in varying circumstances, and with different problems.

YOUR TURN!

THIS WHOLE THING is quite simple, really. It just takes practice. Just as the children learn to refer always to their best selves, so can you. Remember the questions -

Who am I when I like myself?

Who am I when I am the best I can be?

I love the essential me, therefore I love the essential everybody. Once I can love me, knowing and forgiving my foibles and shortcomings, then I can do the same for everybody else.

The children are establishing inner security, a safe vantage point from which to view the world and their place in it.

So can we.

BIOGRAPHIES

Frances Farrer is a writer, broadcaster and journalist who specialises in the subject of children and education. She was on the staff of The Times Educational Supplement for some years and then became a regular freelance contributor to it. Her children's stories have been broadcast on Radio 4, her plays for children played to capacity audiences on the Edinburgh Festival Fringe, and she produced three arts festivals for children on the South Bank in London. She is the biographer of the educationist and spiritual leader, Sir George Trevelyan.

When the full-length version of this book was published, **Neil Hawkes** was head teacher of West Kidlington Primary School, Oxfordshire, where the positive values programme evolved and was put in place. He then worked in the Oxfordshire Education Authority, with a comprehensive brief that included developing a values-based approach to teaching and learning in schools. He is now an international consultant to educators at all levels on values education. The subject formed the core of his doctoral thesis at Oxford University.